Prayer for the twenty-first century

To Sarah and Scott Vickers-Willis, with love

Thomas C. Lothian Pty Ltd
11 Munro Street, Port Melbourne, Victoria 3207

National Library of Australia
Cataloguing-in-Publication data:

Marsden, John, 1950–.
   Prayer for the 21st Century

   ISBN 0 85091 814 6

   I. Title. II. Title: Prayer for the 21st Century

A821.3

Design and graphics by Barbara Beckett and Ann Rosiger
Photo research by Don Chapman
Printed in Hong Kong by Colorcraft Ltd

Acknowledgements

Front cover photograph: Max Dupain, 'Smiling Boy at Glebe, 1939', courtesy of Jill White Photography, Cremorne; NSW; **Jacket photograph of John Marsden:** Lynette Zeeng; **Illustration shown with Line 1, May the road ...:** Lam Dung, 'Voyage', *ARTEXPRESS Catalogue 1996*, courtesy of Board of Studies, NSW (From the ARTEXPRESS Exhibition, an annual exhibition of outstanding works from the Higher School Certificate Visual Arts examination. Presented by the NSW Department of School Education and the Board of Studies, NSW, the exhibition showcases the quality of visual arts education in NSW schools. This work expresses the journey from Vietnam to Australia undertaken by the artist's family, who were boat people); **May it lead ...:** Jessica Shervington, 'The Watchers', *ARTEXPRESS Catalogue 1996*, courtesy of Board of Studies, NSW (from the ARTEXPRESS exhibition); **May the stars ...:** Banapana Maymuru, 'The Stars of the Milky Way', Courtesy of Buku Larrnnggay Art Centre, Yirrkala via Nhulunbuy, **May every aircraft ...:** Ivor Francis, Australia, 1906–1993, 'Antarctic Adventure No. 11: The Wing and I', 1978, oil on canvas on board, 55.0 × 76.5 cm, private collection, courtesy of the Art Gallery of South Australia; **May sailors ...:** *left:* Tadasu Yamamato, Japan, 1950–, 'Allegory 111 (canoe smouldering)', 1988, Siatama, Japan, gelatin-silver photograph, 24.0 × 29.3 cm, Art Gallery of South Australia, gift of Toshikatsu Endo, 1992; *right:* Giacomo Bozzi, 'The Second Miracle', *ARTEXPRESS Catalogue 1996*, courtesy of Board of Studies, NSW (from the ARTEXPRESS exhibition); **May gardens ...:** Mike Slattery, Brighton, SA; **May dangers ...:** David Moore, 'Outback Children—SA—1963'; **May fears ...:** Arthur Boyd, Australia, 1920–, 'Figures by a Creek', oil on canvas on board, 76.2 × 89.0 cm, Art Gallery of South Australia, purchased 1993; **May the mountains ...:** Ansel Adams, United States, 1902–1984, 'Mt Williamson, Sierra Nevada, from Manzanar, California, 1944', gelatin-silver photograph, 39.0 × 46.2 cm, collection of the National Gallery of Australia; **Of what it means ...:** David Strachan, Australia, 1919–1970, 'Lovers and Shell', n.d., oil on canvas, 35.7 × 55.8 cm, L. J. Wilson Bequest Fund, 1972, collection of the Ballarat Fine Art Gallery; **May we be outlived by our daughters:** *left:* Stuart Owen Fox, Mullumbimby, NSW, 'Tjapukai Girl'; *right:* Adam Giles, Salisbury, SA, 'Reflections of Tranquility'; **May we be outlived by our sons:** *left:* Scooter & Jinx, Brighton, SA; *right:* Anahita Johnson, 'Out of the Blue/Into the Black', *ARTEXPRESS Catalogue 1996*, courtesy of Board of Studies, NSW (from the ARTEXPRESS exhibition); **May the bombs ...:** Katharine Nevitt, 'Veni Vedi Vici', *ARTEXPRESS Catalogue 1996*, courtesy of Board of Studies, NSW (from the ARTEXPRESS exhibition); **May the solitary scientists ...:** Weaver Hawkins, 'Atomic Power' 1947, oil on hardboard 61 × 78.5 cm, Art Gallery of New South Wales; **May the knife ...:** Ashley Starkey, Camden Park, SA, 'Guilty of Mayhem?'; **May the bullet ...:** Robyn Stacey, Australia, 1950–, 'Jet', 1988, direct positive colour photograph, 144.0 × 78.9 cm (image), Art Gallery of South Australia, Maude Vizard-Wholohan Art Prize Purchase Award 1990; **May those who live ...:** Max Dupain, 'Thin Man, Newport', courtesy of Jill White Photography, Cremorne, NSW; **Be seen ...:** Max Dupain, 'Sunrise at Newport', courtesy of Jill White Photography, Cremorne, NSW.

Prayer for the twenty-first century

John Marsden

Lothian
BOOKS

May the road be free for the journey,

promised

May it lead where it promised it would,

May the stars that gave ancient bearings

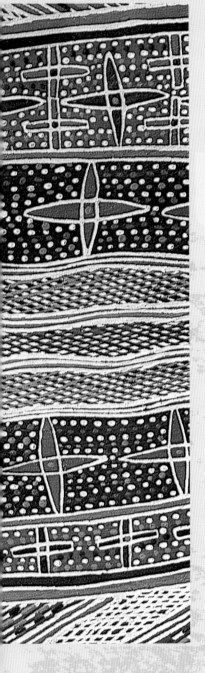

understood

Be seen, still be understood.

safely

May every aircraft fly safely,
May every traveller be found,

cries

May sailors in crossing the ocean
Not hear the cries of the drowned.

wild

May gardens be wild, like jungles,
May nature never be tamed,

heroes

May dangers create of us heroes,

May fears always have names.

remind

May the mountains stand to remind us
Of what it means to be young,

May we be outlived by our daughters,

May we be outlived by our sons.

May the bombs rust away in the bunkers,
And the doomsday clock not be rewound,

remember

May the solitary scientists, working,
Remember the holes in the ground.

May the knife remain in the holder,

May the bullet stay in the gun,

live

May those who live in the shadows
Be seen by those in the sun.

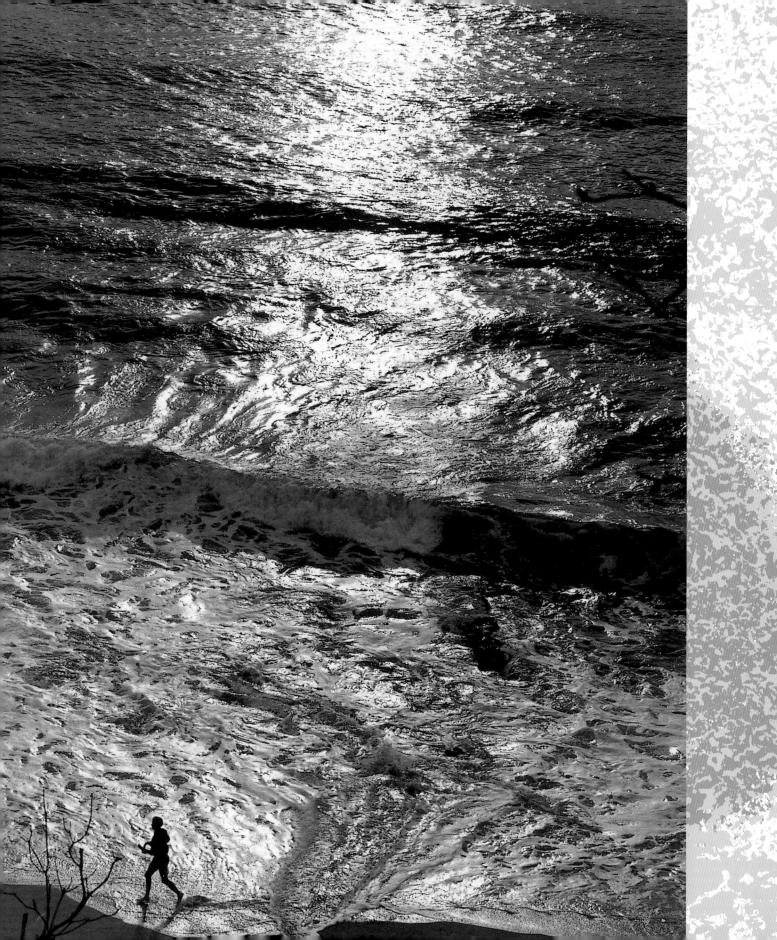

John Marsden

A prayer for the twenty-first century

May the road be free for the journey,
May it lead where it promised it would,
May the stars that gave ancient bearings
Be seen, still be understood.
May every aircraft fly safely,
May every traveller be found,
May sailors in crossing the ocean
Not hear the cries of the drowned.

May gardens be wild, like jungles,
May nature never be tamed,
May dangers create of us heroes,
May fears always have names.
May the mountains stand to remind us
Of what it means to be young,
May we be outlived by our daughters,
May we be outlived by our sons.

May the bombs rust away in the bunkers,
And the doomsday clock not be rewound,
May the solitary scientists, working,
Remember the holes in the ground.
May the knife remain in the holder,
May the bullet stay in the gun,
May those who live in the shadows
Be seen by those in the sun.